From Grief to Glory

Poems for Healing

Annette Toles Young

xulon
PRESS

DEDICATION

This book is dedicated to the memory of four individuals. Their presence in my life was a gift from God.

My husband, Walter Lawrence Young, Sr. (d. 1996)
My father, Will Toles (d.1993)
My mother, Charity Redding Toles (d. 1962)
My niece, Alberta Jones Foster (d. 2006)

ACKNOWLEDGMENTS

I owe a great debt of gratitude to my children, grandchildren, family, friends and St. Peter Baptist Church family, who have prayed for me, loved me and interacted with me during the last eleven years. Thank you for the many ways you showed your love and patience.

Three of my grandchildren wrote remembrances about their grandfather, which were placed in the funeral program. In so doing, they helped lead the way to my being open to expressing my grief by writing this book of poems. In acknowledgment of that, I offer special thanks to Christopher Cole, Thembi Cole and Devon Dudley.

Sincere thanks to book editor, Joann Bradehoft.

Special thanks to Janet and Patricia Toles for their computer expertise in helping me to edit and format my manuscript for submission to the publisher.

Heartfelt thanks to Christel Bonner, Cynthia Cole, John Daniels and Natychia Young for your computer tips and encouragement throughout this process.

Thanks Delores Hill for your special package.

TABLE OF CONTENTS

INTRODUCTION

Have you had a relative or a dear friend who passed away? Maybe it was your child, your spouse, your parent or grandparent, or a sister or brother. Do you remember seeing the heartwrenching photograph taken of the young woman lying face down, atop the grave of her slain fiancée at Arlington National Cemetery (access to photograph available at http://blogs.gettyimages.com/news/2007/05/), in May of 2007? If you, yourself, have suffered the loss of a loved one, you understand that, truly, the picture taken of her is worth a thousand words.

Less than two months before our twenty-sixth wedding anniversary, my husband died. This event marked the beginning of my journey through grief, in an unexpected way.

The story of why and how we grieve is important. So, too, is the story of how we can and should be healed of our grief. Often, the "why" comes from our despair over the loss of our loved one's presence in our life. We may often struggle with the circumstances surrounding their death as much as we do with the fact that we are powerless to alter the events. Ultimately, we realize that the real task at hand is to determine how we will navigate our way through a journey we never wished to embark upon.

We find ourselves wondering why we could not have had one more meaningful conversation. There are conversations that were started that we didn't have a chance to finish. Other conversations we didn't even have a chance to begin. Many more conversations we now know we should have had, that we had never even thought about.

It is my hope that this book will prove a worthy companion to travel with you through what might seem the darkest time in your life. The author's desire is to address how we can grieve in order to experience healing. This book does not question why. It does not question how long. It does not question when or where. It does not question the sovereignty of God.

The book does seek to address the tendency to avoid talking about the pain of grief. Too many people believe that by changing the subject and not talking about the debilitating sadness of grief, it will just go away. Nothing could be further from the truth. The terror faced by those who grieve is perpetrated by an evil enemy. It is the same enemy faced by Job. Notice that the word of God does not say that Job, being a righteous man, did not grieve. Indeed this book in the Bible contains forty-two chapters that cover the five basic stages of grieving. The generally agreed upon stages of grieving include denial, anger, bargaining, depression, and acceptance. (An article listing and describing the stages may be accessed at http://mt.essortment.com/stagesofgri_rvg.htm.)

The proverbial "light at the end of the tunnel" centers around maintaining faith in God in the midst of our grief. Finding out how to grieve exhibits our faith and not the lack thereof. As with Job, if our sovereign God, in His loving providence allows us to experience grief, then He is there to assist us through our grief. For the author of this book, that's how these poems came to be.

The poems became a method whereby various heart-wrenching emotions could be voiced through words to release the pain within. Consider this actual occurrence as an example of how I was guided to use the words that flooded my mind when confronted with the many difficulties which face all those who grieve. One day while driving to an exercise class, I was preparing to stop at a traffic light that had just turned red. Almost immediately my mind took the momentary stop to begin pondering four major decisions I needed to make about some really serious matters. Suddenly before I could think through one of these issues, I heard myself say, "I am defeated."

Just then, the wheels started turning again and another poem began to form in my mind. I took out my pad and jotted down the key words. Then and there I knew this would be a poem about admitting that I was experiencing the emotion of defeat. But I also knew that I had to travel through this rough spot. Laying it all out in a poem would help. By simply writing the word 'defeated' in the poem, I would acknowledge that such thoughts were present. Then that line would be followed with other words that would express how I would survive the issues at hand and not allow them to conquer me. This poem about feeling defeated began as follows:

The Failure of Defeat

Seems impossible to think and believe.
Could be a lie that a weary mind would conceive.
Defeated again where there seems no way to win.
Why propose another breath and turn away eternal rest.
The lie exists but not in the truth.
Remember the day when darkness hailed you and you
    answered no.
Find triumph anew as often as you must.
Refresh some formulas. Create others unknown.
Success upon failure always sits alone.

At the end of the poem, you find yourself regaining optimism. You are strengthened to reassert your ability and desire to overcome adversity. The author admits that the feeling of being defeated was present and almost triumphed. That's what the fourth line indicates when it speaks of just wanting to die and go to eternal rest. But in the succeeding lines, we are reminded of past successes and become "determined" instead to refresh ourselves for battle and expect more triumphs.

The last line of "The Failure of Defeat" presents the idea that failure will be present but success will come and have a place of honor. No one gives a special seat to failure. The line says that success sits alone; failures are to be dumped together in one heap. When you walk into a school's gym where the banners of championship years are on display, only the team's triumphs are shown. You don't see a display honoring non-championship years. This thought brings to mind a powerful verse of scripture. "Oh death where is thy sting? Oh grave where is thy victory?" (I Corinthians 15:55).

One evening, while explaining to a friend the need to compile my poems into a book, I shared this revelation. The poems came at me as if they were on the wings of words. These were words that revealed the weight of emotions associated with grief. The image was comparable to looking through a window and seeing words flying by as if to say, "Hi, this is what you are experiencing at this moment. See us, feel us, touch us, put us all together."

Using the essence of these words, I would then undertake the task of stringing them together for the best portrayal of the way my soul had been touched. It was as if I grabbed at them, and arranged them and rearranged them, within the frame of a window into which I had been gazing. Sometimes the window was dark (as though it was night), and so was the message of the poem. At other times, more light shined in and the view was clearer. Still others were written in windows of bright, promising light. This method of using poetry became my attempt to give an accurate and concise view of the scene inside my heart where my emotions were twisting and gnawing away at my very being.

And so went the process by which emotions were recorded, acknowledged, and released within the lines of my poetry. No longer were they hiding within, eating away at me. I could go back in an instant, open the window of a poem, and see all there was to see about the raw emotion of a day or an event. I could just as easily review or relive how I overcame the troubling circumstance. And especially how I made the transition to adopt a new lifestyle. I was able to look back and see my progression through the stages of grief. This became a strategy that gave me the strength and reassurance I needed to heal. I even sensed that if I tried to skip a particular poem that was coming to me by not writing it down, I would eventually have to endure the full force of that stage of grief."

My poems are offered as a personal service to others who want a more manageable journey through grief. Write notes in the margins beside the poems. You may simply write "yes", I had that happen to me or "yes", I feel that way. Perhaps different words will come to you that pinpoint your own emotions. Discover the best method for you to write them down as a way to reach into your soul to help pull out the pain. Your technique may be to compose a song, journal, create a scrapbook of pictures with captions, or even write your own poetry. Use the progressive sequence of the chapter titles in this book to help identify your current stage of grief. Allow them to help you confirm that you are moving toward healing. If you feel led to create your own project, employ grief sequencing as a part of the process.

By all means find a way to avoid allowing the pain of grief to run rampant and wreak havoc, leaving in its wake unending sorrow and depression. That's not what our loved ones would want. That's not what God wants. Peace, Love and Hope in the Resurrection. "... I am the resurrection, and the life: he that believeth in me, though he were dead, yet shall he live: And whosoever liveth and believeth in me shall never die...." (John 11:25-26).

Chapter One

RAW GRIEF

This chapter includes some of the earliest poems written following the death of my husband. These poems cover the period that I refer to as a time of Raw Grief. At first, raw grief can be overwhelming, as you will gather from the poems in this chapter. Some of the poems show evidence of anger, faith under attack, guilt about not being able to stop death, or sadness about missed opportunities to love more powerfully and unconditionally. At the moment when death steals our loved one away, we find ourselves caught off guard. Our loved one moves and speaks no more on this side.

Although we know that death often comes without warning, and we are powerless to prevent it, this does very little to ease our suffering. Whether it is tragic and unexpected, as in the Virginia Tech shootings, or after a period of illness, the response is the same.

Consider the circumstances surrounding the death and resurrection of Lazarus. Lazarus had been ill. He didn't get well and he died.

Jesus arrived four days later. Mary and Martha, Lazarus' two sisters, were in great sorrow. While their brother had lain ill, they had sent for Jesus. Jesus had tarried. This was an event that Jesus would use to show His resurrection power to the disciples and all who believe. It would forever become a picture of how mere man, through Jesus, will triumph over the suffering and grief caused by our old enemy, death.

In the eleventh chapter of John, two emotions expressed by Jesus are revealed which I feel demonstrate His understanding of our tears and sorrow. In verse thirty-three, it states that Jesus groaned when he saw Mary and the Jews with her weeping. In verse thirty-five, it states that Jesus, himself, wept. Additionally, in verse thirty-eight, we read the following: "Jesus therefore again groaning in himself cometh to the grave... " It's important to stop and note that in verse thirty-six, the Jews who were present made an important observation. They saw Jesus weeping. The scripture says they stated, "... Behold how he loved him!" God cares and knows how death creates deep sorrow in our hearts.

At first the pain of sorrow may be quite raw, as disclosed in the poems in the first chapter. The process of expressing that sorrow through these poems captures runaway emotions. This outpouring of sentiment helps to refocus energy on the promises of God. Indeed, it ignites a hunger to search through the scriptures for reassurance. It leads to openness and true expression in one's prayers. We sense that God does not expect us to hold back the questions we may have or the tears we must shed. He wants us to have an honest dialogue, as would a child and loving father who would cradle us in his arms and encourage us to release our fears.

DEAR TEARS

Never another tear so dear.
Never another tear so near.
Never another heart to be broken.
Just this once, that's the rule unspoken.

Never caring again.
Never sharing what must end.
Never room for more such pain.
Never, ever to love again.

Sit and think for a long, long while.
Cover it up with a smile.
Choose the decor for others to view.
Never over, death's not through.
People are dying today who never died before.
There's always a journey walking through the door.

Hush, hush, shut your door.
Death always comes back for more.
Can't close this door; it's been opened wide.
No place to run, no place to hide.
Once broken, once opened, once in.
Life knows, yes, death wins.

No, stop. Remember that all hope is not lost.
Victory over death was achieved at Calvary's cross.
So put an X on that thought.
For you're a treasure paid and bought.

ROBBED

A thief came.
He's one and the same.
A thief came.
Do you know his name?
He left in the night.
Oh, it's death.
Comes by night, comes by day.
The results are the same, and then he goes away.

First comes to stare.
Second comes to dare.
Third comes unaware.
Such a thief; He defies belief!
Leaves only one thing: a share of pity and grief.

THIS IS PAIN!

Pain in, pain out, pain no more. No more pain, when?
Pain down, pain up, pain around. Pain around, when?
Pain above, pain below, no pain. No pain, when?
Pain beside, pain inside, pain outside. Pain outside, when?
Ask another question. Take another chance.
This is pain even at a glance.

Come stand with me in this land where a widow stands.
No, don't come. You will come. It will come, this pain.
Unbidden; it comes.
This is pain's land. Here pain takes a stand.
Bow down low, low, low and more.
Cry rivers full, full, and fuller still.
The cold wind blows, and the pain grows.
Hot and sunny, cold and lonely, this is pain.
No way of escaping.

It comes from outside in, from around to in,
From down to in, from above to in, from distant to in,
From thin to in, from wide to in, from beside to in,
From below to in, from above to in.
Can't fight it off.
Can't outrun it.
Can't cry it away.
Can only bow below the might of this grief.
In, in.
Searing pain, this is pain.
Excruciating as the point of a sharp and gleaming arrow.
Piercing flesh, bone and marrow.
A swift and bold move and it's in.

I CRY

I hurt all over. I cry.
No eye is dry. Day or night. Dark or bright.
I hurt all over. I cry.
Fuller than life and that's now gone.
Sad as sorrow, I'm so alone.
I hurt all over. I cry

No eye is dry. Day or night. Dark or bright.
I hurt with gripping pain.
I am not ashamed, for I loved with a caretaker's love.
It's just the pain, the human pain.
Letting depression in now.
Letting doubt float about.
This way in, no way out.
Last night I didn't cry.

The night before, I did.
The night before then?
Okay, okay you win.
I cried in my sleep.

I longed for and there was no end
I hurt all over.
I cry, I cry, I cry.
Wrap me in your arms and hold me close, Lord.
Father, I need you deep in my soul.
This pain of sorrow is ever so bold.
Yes, I cry to you, Lord, and you look into my eyes.
You say don't be ashamed, I gave you tears, my child.

MAD

Fell down as you moved up.
Each turn of the wheel takes me to a place I don't want to
    go.
Unknown, forlorn and without you.
Tired of crying, thinking about dying.
Mad, angry, sad, no lie, this is bad.
Crushed, shocked, can't perceive a clear thought.
Angry, sad, and very mad.

Mad at that serpent from hell.
Too mad to tell.
Not near glad.
Don't come near me.
Why now?
Why not later?
Much, much later.

Do not give answers.
Hate those answers.
Mad about those answers.
Sad about those answers.
Yes, it happens every day.
But somewhere else. Why did it come this way?
Answer the question with the answer you know.
Nobody bids death in at the door.
It comes unannounced in minutes and seconds.
It arrives as a guest highly unwelcome.
Cry some more.
Maybe one in a million tears holds the antidote.
Every day is another day.
Distance that keeps getting farther away.
Reach out and grab.
Try to hold on.

Hands have slipped their bounds and fingertips groan.
Remember the hold; remember and grow old.
Can't imagine this anger ever being over.
They say one day memories will win.
Not glad, but joy and understanding, will return.
Treasured memories will fill the void.
A fresh newness will come and mend a broken heart.
It waits for the moment.
The patience within its boundaries does triumph.
For the present it's okay to be angry, sad and mad.
Vent such pain.
Holding it inside, yields nothing of gain.

SING A SONG ANOTHER DAY

Another day has come.
Another annual day is here.
Another year has passed.
Yet this pain lasts.
Can't express joy.
Can't let happiness in.
Can't sing a song.
Don't wish to begin again.
How do I sing a song now?
Why would I sing a song now?
Wouldn't be fair.
We never talked about a song to sing when one of us was
    no longer there.
We never talked about a song to sing when for life we no
    longer care.
Can only remember our song, "A Band of Gold."
Only want to sing that song but can't grab hold.
Can't pretend to go on.
The band is broken.
Just can't bear to know gladness and go on.
When death has spoken.
Just want to mourn and moan in deep pain.
Giving in to the pain, which washes in like pouring rain.
Rolls in to soak and maintain the insane.
Follow this storm to the rainbow's end.
Golden is the story that one day will win.
Not the gold in the band from the song.
But the golden strength found in the Savior's arms.

Still can't sing now.
Believe, for there is a way.
All who mourn can sing a song another day.

YELL

What did I yell that day?
What didn't I yell that day?
What should I have yelled that day?
What could I have yelled that day?
What I wish I had yelled that day!
That I had yelled and yelled and let time tell.

Yell that day.
Tell that day.
Wail that day.
Mourn that day.
Cry that day.
And then yell and yell and yell.
That day owns center stage.
That day comes as strong-armed tears.
Never knew tears signaled that you are breaking apart.
Thought they were tender signals of a broken heart.

That day yells messages before ignored, but then so
      clear.
That day yells life's a precious treasure.
Do tell others to hold it dear.
Cherish it now.
Yell it later.
That day.

PIECES

My heart is broken in two.
One for me, one for you.
When you left, one half was torn to go.
The other half crumbled into pieces for evermore.
Somehow I know you say to me, mend.
Rearrange the pieces and it will enlarge with the rays of
    love you send.
A new configuration born from loss and pain.
An assigned duty to live, an assigned hope to gain.
But the pieces of my heart beat in pain!
These torn pieces are simply not meant to rise again.

Trying to rise is another side to this story.
A line desires to be written full of fame and pictures of
    glory.
Resources absent to make real that tale.
Hear again what grieving verses do repeat.
My heart was yours, so it left with you.
There's something in its place that's painfully hollow and
    new.
Again glory falters, stutters and halts.
Truly this blow was meant to pierce and alter from the very
    start.
How much sadness can a heart know?
How much sadness can a heart hold?
How much sadness can a life alone grow?
How much sadness do I truly know?
Or is it that sadness knows me?
It knows where I live. It came to visit. It intends to stay.
Oh God, please God, make it go away!
It's not my friend, nor my kin, just my end if I fail this test
    to mend.

FRIEND

Never imagined that one more day you would not know.
Never imagined that one more day you would not grow.
Never imagined that I could one day be alone.
Never imagined that sorrow would occupy and crowd my
home.
And then again, I never imagined life without you, my
friend.
Never imagined all these ever flowing tears.
Never imagined the lonely passing of the years.
Never imagined or thought I could,
Think, then cry, then sit, then lie, then fall, then crawl,
Then moan, then scream, then ache with pain ever so mean.
That passion no longer exists in my life's scenes.
And then again, I never imagined life without you, my
friend.

They say plan. Talk to the insurance man.
What does he know? What can he show?
Just paper and lines with legal binds.
We never imagined what he didn't know.
Does anyone imagine that he's just part of a cruel show?
When the curtain is closed, and the lid is locked,
I never imagined that there exists no clause, nor any pause
to the pain I feel,
For I never imagined life without you, my friend, could
become real.

DREAM INVASION

Sleep disturbed again by these visions swirling in my head,
Here in the land of the living, they come visiting from the
    land of the dead.
In this dream, death is a woman, not a man.
Boldly she saunters in and steals loved ones from the
    grasps of our hands.
Now she brings a nightmare that says they loved us less.
She spins a tale of their going away to roam for adventure
    and not for eternal rest.

Try hard to remember the author of these lines.
Even when sleep is disturbed with dreams of sorrow
    sublime.
Satan writes another Question to make us thirst,
Always creating confusion as he has from the very first.

MOMENTS

There were moments not treasured, moments not measured.
No way they'll come back.
No days to heal the slack.
Time's gone, days too.
The chance to dig for deep treasure and be thankful for you.

Shine on gold. Gleam silver.
Dazzle brilliant emeralds, rubies and pearls.
But none matter without you in this world.

Such brilliance cannot satisfy.
Not in the midst of tears flowing from each eye.
Only one chest of treasure and it has grown cold.
Oh God, please rescue our souls.
Give us a chance again our treasure to hold.
No. The moment is over.
All that's left, is to tell what you've been told.

Chapter Two

IN THE MIDST OF TEARS

This next chapter of poems covers the period I termed, "In the Midst of Tears." It was a time when for no apparent reason, tears would begin falling from my eyes. That is when I knew it was time to create a new way to live my life. So despite prolonged reluctance and tear-filled days, it was still a period when things seemed to be getting more manageable.

Unfortunately, it was also a period marked by unbelievable human behavior leading to even more tears. I was sickened to discover how unscrupulous some individuals could be in their business dealings with a widow. For example, after repeatedly promising (and then failing), to repair my heating system (in the dead of winter), one repairman finally admitted he had just been "giving me the runaround!" He had always followed through and kept his appointments when my husband was alive. Why did he suddenly become so different? It made that period in my life scary because I didn't know who to call to make house or car repairs. My husband had always handled these matters and now I was at a loss as to who to trust. As a result, I made many mistakes trying to hire people to perform such work. Once again, I found myself in tears from having trusted the wrong people and because I was alone, and because I was experiencing the world as I had never imagined.

When I talked to other widows, they had similar stories to tell. A lot of these stories I heard from widows whom I met by chance while out shopping. Something about our demeanor must have signaled our kindred grief. Once we knew we had widowhood in common, we would often spend time sharing the horror stories of our newfound existence. We knew the other person would listen and understand our need to vent our feelings.

We listened and showed that we cared, even though we realized we would probably never see each other again. For a few minutes, we were able to empathize with one another and offer comfort and advice. We knew all too well how much the other person needed encouragement and an understanding ear to battle the adversary of persecution and loneliness which preys on widows.

When the tears won't stop flowing, and daily tasks await you at the dawning of each new day, you may wonder if tears are a part of you or if you are a part of tears. They seem to express so power-fully the dramatic change in your life. Recording my grief in poetry helped to ease the suffocating pain and confusion of this time. The process sustained me as I continued to reach out to God. I was deter-mined not to allow this event to separate me from the love God has for me as well as my love for Him.

The verses of scripture that helped me sustain my belief through my tears come from the book of Romans. "Who shall separate us from the love of Christ? Shall tribulation, or distress, or persecution, or famine, or nakedness, or peril, or sword?" For I am persuaded that neither death, nor life, nor angels, nor principalities, nor powers, nor things present, nor things to come, Nor height, nor depth, nor any other creature, shall be able to separate us from the love of God, which is in Christ Jesus our Lord" (Romans 8:35, 38, 39).

For me this was a time of almost relentless crying. Through the poems that were flowing through my head and onto paper, I made an important discovery. I had been given a strategy to help clear the clutter of cascading and painful emotions during this period full of tribulation, grief, persecution and distress. The expressions in each line of poetry would actually help me analyze what was happening to me. During the writing process, the cause of the tears, the need to eliminate Satan's ability to triumph in his taunting and the need to totally and submissively focus on my faith in God became evident. Seeing on paper the battle raging inside, helped to keep me connected to a loving heavenly Father. I believe these poems will do the same for anyone experiencing similar grief. What the poems reveal, through faith we know, only God in his omnipotence and omniscience can heal.

TEARS KNOW

Tears are for crying, crying for the living, crying for the
dying.
Ever flowing, ever growing, wet, heavy, ever knowing.
Tears know the time, the place, the moment.
Tears see the pain inside gnawing and growing.
Tears hear the sob, deep at its birth.
Tears know the heart when it holds no mirth.
Tears express, speak, and vent.
They cry anger, hurt, pain, sad times, hard times, low times,
pain, searing pain.
Yes, tears express and tears explain.
Not just water, not just wet.
Their true nature not fully discovered, no not yet.
Mysteries they remain.
Until all well spent, they don't change.
They become the nearest friend, the dearest friend, the
knowing and the bravest friend.
Spend time with tears for time well spent.
Spend time with tears.
They know and show where life has been spent.
They count the years, the months, the weeks, the days, the
hours, the minutes, the seconds.
Count the sum of all those drops.
Wet. Heavy water bursting forth and unashamed to never
stop.
You really want to know what I feel, how I feel, why I'm
sad, why I cry?
I know the answers. I know them all too well.
But the best at responding through this pain would not be
me even after all these years.
Ask the great wise ones. Ask the tears.

CRYING AGAIN

Crying tears to fill rivers.
Rivers that are full.
Rivers washed over and from my face.
From my eyes, such a disgrace.
No, not what they said, but what they thought.
If they only knew how I can see through the tale they
    brought.
So I am crying again.
Yes, again.
It hurts.

I cry. Yes, I even ask why.
Yes, again.
You need to hush. You need to go away.
You have no wisdom, for you have no day.
You have no tears which have come to stay.
You have no loss. You bear no cross.

Have you a river?
Oh yes, I too, see that pool.
Try not to forget that you're en route, on your way to
    school.
One day, you might arrive.
You, too, might grow wise when rivers wash over your face
    pouring down from your eyes.
Don't wish for that. It's not a friendly pat.
Just old trouble which comes on the double.
Hush now. Go away. Find more joy and fill your day.

THE WIDOW'S EYES

As she was leaving to go, she stopped and turned to look at
 me as she stood beside the frame of the door.
I looked at her as she was looking at me.
In her eyes I saw that she knew more than at that moment I
 could see.
Too many people were present for such personal tales to be
 given sound.
By her silent movement across the threshold she was
 bound.

Her pain had long been there.
The tears welling in her eyes revealed unspoken care.
She knew that now I too might not be free.
Her eyes expressed her pity for me.
Look into my eyes she seemed to be saying and focus on
 their silent message.
Comprehend the beginning of your story.

If only she could have pulled me aside.
Would she have spoken words or shared in the brimming
 watershed of tears wanting to spill from my eyes?
As for words, it probably was still too early for ears newly
 attuned to grief to have really heard.

She knew the magnitude and strength of the pain from
 which I would recoil.
I read the silent prayer in her eyes for me.
"May God bless and keep you," the older widow seemed to
 say with a sad smile.

"God knows that you are just starting on this painful
    journey of too many miles.
It is His peace and comfort that will transport you when
    you are lonely.
Cry, for you must. Don't hold back.

Sob through your sorrow to lighten your heavy heart.
Don't try to stop the swift, raging, and numbing tide.
Tears will ease the pain that you will feel inside.
They function as releases of the feverish heat of grief.
Though sometimes the pain only steps away for a brief
    retreat.
At other times, such freedom may last for a long hour or a
    day.
The surging waves of pain will come, washing over you
    and hampering your way.
Strange, but you sometimes will welcome it close.
It's the company that you keep, for it replaced the one for
    whom you weep.
The time will come.
You will again find the spirit to reach.
Reach for it. Reach! Reach! Reach!
Don't let go. Hold it close and you, too, will know.
Why the tears, though fewer in number, still fall from my
    eyes.
You'll understand why I cry without disguise.
Cry, for you must. Don't hold back.
On the other side of this pain, the grace of the tears conduct
    you to your level of sane."

CHARACTERS

There are characters who walk in and characters who walk
    out.
Some characters say, "It'll soon be over."
Others say, "You'll get better."
Still others say, "Get up and get out."
Some characters say, "I hear your moan."
There are still others who say, "I know your groan."
Many say, "Today, for you I pray."
The best say, "My prayers will continually ascend for you,
For I know grief desires to make an end of you."

They are all characters called to this stage.
They listen for their cue in this sad parade.
Sobs they hear.
Tears they see.
Most come forth and offer good cheer.
But when the curtain rolls down and the lights are dark,
In this scene, they have no part.
The sound of the sobs and tears fall on lonely, weary ears.

Listen, there is a prayer ascending.
It's coming from the character whose knee is still bending.

POWER

I've tried to live this one day at a time.
Then along comes a power that knocks me behind.
The power of a memory, the power of a scene.
The power of a meal, the power in a dream.
The power of a thought about what needs to be done.
The power that says now you're the only one.
So much power brought to bear. Was there this much
    power times two to share?
Probably one half power for me, and the other half for
    you.

It's spirit-breaking to have to perform the daily tasks
    and try to go on.
It's heart-breaking to try to stand as one for two, and
    then be strong.
I smile though it's no longer sunny.
One of the toughest things to do.
Alone now, trying to find the other part of me that was
    you.
Somehow I hear at a distance, a rich and clear voice.
Speaking words which clearly announce a new choice.
Let your smile find and cherish the power in you.
No need to doubt this thing that's old, tried and true.
Power everlasting designed for those going through.

THE FAILURE OF DEFEAT

Seems impossible to think and believe.
Could be a lie that for a weary mind that evil serpent would
conceive.
Defeated again where there seems no way to win.
Why propose another breath and turn away eternal rest?
The lie exists but not in the truth.
Remember the day when darkness hailed you and you
answered no.
Find triumph anew as often as you must.
Refresh some formulas. Create others unknown.
Success upon failure always sits alone.

When did God tell you never to cry?
Why was there a need for Jesus to dry his eye?
At Lazarus' tomb he stood.
Weeping and groaning as did many in the neighborhood.

Our thoughts are not taller.
Our ways are not broader.
Nor are they equal.
High above, He does see what it is that we need.
Ready and willing, fail not to admit that it is He we must
heed.
Never exchange the truth of God's love, for Satan's lies.
Keep a proper focus. On the cross, center our eyes.

PROGRAMMED

Paying that bill; not on my program.
Checking rear tail lights; not on my program.
Listening to the plumbing pipes; not on my program.
Looking at the pipes beneath sinks; not on my program.
Watching the sway of the trees to know the health of their
    leaves; not on my program.
Pulling and checking the dog's ears; not on my program.
Loving through the years; on my program.
Kicking the car tires; not on my program.
Changing the oil and filters in the car; not on my program.
Washing and waxing the car; not on my program.
Climbing onto and checking the roof; not on my program.
Stepping onto and listening for possible creaks in the steps;
    not on my program.
Staring at light globes; not on my program.
Removing light switch covers, to check the wiring; not on
    my program.
Missing the care and glow of love; now on my program.
Overwhelmed and crying; a program update.

MAKING FOOLISH DECISIONS

Buying, Selling, Trying, Not telling.
Don't know. Don't ask.
Wonder who knows. Wonder who cares.
Didn't ask the pastor.
Did ask, but too much later.
Wouldn't ask a friend.
Making foolish decisions end over end, and again and
    again.
Who cares? Who has time to know? Who even dares step
    close?
Hired the wrong carpenter.
Called the wrong air conditioner repairman.
Let the worst painter into the house.
Trusted a fast-talking landscaper, who could scam a louse.

Trying to go it alone because alone is the reality.
The reality with which this mind thinks it must now learn
    to survive.
There exists no quick book of few pages.
No one stands ready planting yellow bricks to outline the
    way.
Do this tomorrow; do this today.

No clue given, nor understood, that the thinking cap is now
    on half a woman or half a man.
Why do people not know what to say, what to do?
Why can't they see in between the lines of the smile, the
    puff of the tear stained eyes?
Say out loud, if the sink needs fixing, let me know.
If the heat goes out, knock on my door.
Pick up the phone. I'll be home.
The car sounds funny? Come, let's go see what we can do.
I know an honest mechanic. I'll give him a call.

We'll get it towed.
Don't worry. Somewhere there's money that's stored.
No, I don't have a fat bank account now.
Fat bank accounts start long before now and they grow.
Not many understand beforehand; not many really know.
How to plan and not consider such planning taboo.
Add the expenses and then multiply by two. Then triple for
    the unforeseen.
No, that's not mean. That's one of the troubles with this
    scene.
Not listening, not wanting to admit that one day one walks
    alone and the other walks away.
Now decisions galore, that you can no longer ignore.

Many look on and keep score, not understanding where
    your mind must go.
Decisions great, decisions small, some crumbling, many
    causing a great fall.
It springs from the stress of grief, gripping pain so
    consuming, while daily life pursues you.
Time spent weeping and wasted in vain should have been
    used to save your name.

Oh well, it's over and done. Count up the cost and move
    on.
Some minuses, some pluses.
Others don't revisit; just call those hushes.
Go on now. You're getting better at this.
Only the greatest decisions remain to be made.
From the lessons learned which ones must you not trade?

ROLLBACK

Please, I beg, let me roll back time.
Please, I cry, let me just this once.
Please, I plead, let me go back in time and then I'll return.
Please, I beg, let the days before that day come again.
Please, I cry, I'll know better how to make things right, just
    give me one more time, even a night.
Please, I plead, reverse this event.
Make it go away as time not spent.
Can't we pretend that it was just a really bad dream?
Why can't we just pretend it never happened and hide it
    between a magical seam?
Hem it in; don't let it out. Leave this garment in a closet,
    never to be worn about.

Rewrite this whole scene as one from a play.
Erase it and write it out. Make it go away.
Surely you can change the characters, change the storyline,
    change the setting.
Please hear me out, can't you understand all the things I'm
    regretting?

This time, everything will be said that should be said, in the
    way that I now know it in my head.
This time, there'll not be one stone left unturned. Things
    will be done that should be done.
This time, the curtain will go up and the play will go on and
    on in an excellent way.
This time, grant me my wish and let this love one stay.

What did you whisper?
They don't want to come this way again?
They're waiting around a golden bend?

Where rainbows shed light into the sky, where the greetings
    are howdy and never goodbye.
Who's clapping and singing?
All of them?
Then roll back the curtain and let me see, where my heart
    can be free.
Let me see where worry and care cease their fate and
    nothing is ever too late.
Rolling back the curtain is all about time? And that I'll
    know when it's mine?
Then let me remember what a little child said, as he
    pictured his grandad in his head.
Granddaddy Young, up there singing, "If You are Happy
    and You Know it Clap Your Hands."
You, down there, stop your crying. Time has come to get
    up and stand.
Dry your eyes and gird up your loins.
The missions you're on are battles to be won.
Many know not in the reality of life that this day will come
    as a thief in the night.
Tell them. Warn them. Urge them on, to seek and find
    peace and home.

Chapter Three

LOOKING UP AND LOOKING OUT

A journey through grief can make us more deeply aware of the suffering around us. It can cause us to search for ways to express that enlightenment. And so it was that I noticed my poetry becoming less about me and more about what was happening to other people. My own grief taught me that in some way, for people in pain around the world, I needed to care about their sorrow, too. That is why this section of poems is entitled "Looking Up and Looking Out."

The idea is that my bowed head needed to be raised. I stopped looking inside myself and realized that beyond me there is a whole world hurting.

On the news, we hear about the places, the people of these places, the violence or the natural disasters. We see the faces and the destruction. We must not see and look away. We must not hear and not do. And so it is that these poems begin to address national and world events. They highlight some of what we, as a world community of believers, might focus on as we prayerfully engage in efforts to help alleviate the suffering. For this chapter, I selected the following scripture verse. "Remember them that are in bonds, as bound with them; and them which suffer adversity, as being your-selves also in the body" (Hebrews 13:3).

CRY FOR OTHERS

Today I cried many tears.
For a change, they were different from those of many years.
Sure, the tears were still mine.
Yet somehow they knew it was now time.
Time to cry for others and their loss.
The child who drove drunk and lost a friend.
A family whose soldier died far away.
In a land about which we don't know what to say.
A teen caught in a crossfire.
Much too young, such a senseless way to die.
Another teen whose heart they say gave out.
Just trying to have fun and play about.

A young girl's family wondered where she went.
Then it's discovered that some other young folks took her
    life.
They just wanted to see how life looked when it ebbed and
    breath was spent.
A sad young man who hatched a diabolical plan.
Carried it out according to his silent wave of thinking, with
    guns in hand.
Ruthless, cruel, foolish, cold, bold, evil, sinful, hateful,
    uncaring, not them.
Lacking love or missing that which was given.
They won't let you know in this pain, they, too, will be
    sharing.
Putting on that "front." Putting on that "strut."
Not really big, just way too much.

Still crying tears, I now begin to feel the heal.
Look out and look up and understand that others are
    suffering.
Never a day when we grieve alone.
Many tears flow in many homes.
So today, I cry and I pray. "Lord, please show us the way."
The way to live with ourselves.
The way to cease divisions and strife.
The way to let love abide in this life.

ONE BY ONE

The red, the yellow, the white, the black, the grey, the
    brown, none sticks around.
One goes away, they all go away.
One by one in the same day.
Some at the same moment in time.
Just a line in a rhyme.
Truly one by one as it is day by day.
Moment by moment sharing a point in time, sharing a
    line in a rhyme.
Short and tall.
Skinny and round.
Fat and sound.
Young and old.
Middle of the road.
Intelligent and smart.
Challenged and full of heart.
Saved and unsaved.
One by one.
At peace, at rest.
Troubled, not blessed.
Wise, foolish.
Safe and unsafe.
One by one.
Go down, go up.

COUNTING CROSSES AND STARS

In a triangle box, the stars are shown.
In other triangle boxes similar sacrifices are also known.
One set of stars from a long-lived life, the others from a
    young life they did give.
Not something new. Just something old and back again.
Another war, never a win.
Oh maybe, yes maybe, for the moment.
Without the love that beats the weapons into plowshares,
    it's not a win.
Just more stars at which to stare again and again.
Proof lies in the earth.
Cross one, cross two.
Keep counting, not through.
Cross three, cross four.
Keep adding just one more.
Cross seven, cross eight.
Stop, stop. Please wait.
Where is six?
Count the points on the star.
Keep counting, the line lies far.
Cross nine, Cross ten.
When? Say when.
Never, not now.
That answer is not heard.
Dying today as so many before.
Lying beneath a cross.
Now count twenty four.

RAGING

Battles raging.
One spiritual.
One physical.
Who's right?
Who's wrong?
Trying to tell, but taking too long.
Listening to the powers, not of flesh and blood.
Failing to stop and pray, and sing songs we have heard.

Years and years of flowing tears.
Widows, orphans growing and growing.
Many die young, more die old.
Who snuffed the candle that lights the way from this
    cold?
What and where in that heart do you win?
To rule you say, but you lose more each day.
Blood flows by pints, by quarts, by gallons, by barrels
    in graves, many shallow.

And more widows grow and more orphans know when
    you win you lose.
When you lose, you choose.
You choose pain and suffering.
You choose to leave love alone.
You choose to abandon merry little eyes.
You choose to bequeath weariness and sighs.

But who listens, who knows?
Seems no one, but they all do.
They truly lack courage to say that which is true.
Rather lie, than ask, "Who knows the way out?"
Too many ask and find the way in.
It's a sin to make so many cry, cry, and cry again.

The ones you said you'd pave the way for and leave a
    future to.
They see you and tomorrow it's all new.
Of course you say what's through is through.
Not really.
Try to wash your hands. Do the same as the king.
Why do you lie to yourself?
This will be no hidden thing.

PAIN OF MY SISTER

My sister in pain, a whole world away.
I heard about you again today.
It was reported that the bombs went off and the big guns
    fired, too.
Leaving you standing alone and out of view.
Can't look back; there's tomorrow.
Carry on as we pray you through your sorrow.
We're your sisters in pain a distant world away.
It took us a while to know what to say.
We bow now and we do pray.
We know your pain that has come from the grim reaper.
With that unquenchable boldness he pleasures to slay.
He holds and dangles men as his puppets of prey.
They jump and satisfy him while we yell, "Stuff it!"
Stuff the ego and the bravado, too.
You didn't really win.
No one left wins. The headline is true.
A billion down and counting.
When it's over, no one wise to enjoy.
It's now all left up to girls and boys.

Pray for the children and seat them side by side.
Step back and let them hold hands.
Let them decide.
Hopefully, they'll remember the tears we have cried.
Hopefully, they'll remedy the pain inside.

My sister in pain, I pray for you today.
I know not your name but I share in the horror you did not
    wish to gain.
So alone you must feel, and so unsure.
So lost in what is new and what is true.
It hurts everywhere and it will not go away.

It won't allow you to step back or go back, not even for a
    day.
This pain says there is no other way.
Yet we keep looking, thinking and wondering.
At the same time, you must go on and not know where.
Mentioning how is only in your soul.
You must make it happen. You must, even though you
    grow old.
You can because I am not the only one praying.
We pray one for the other.
We know this pain rips further and further.
So far or near, my sister, please hear my prayer for you.
Please accept the love of my prayer and know this that is
    true:
I feel your pain and the intensity of each pestilent grain that
    desires to make you insane.
Don't go that way. Step tall and step it back.
The you that you are made from, does not come from slack.

Fear not fear. Trod it under.
Though the tears flow, let the water know.
Its only purpose is to come, wash and ease the pain away.
The fears may not conquer, for your permission you do not
    give.
I am not the only one praying and giving that you might
    live.
Gather your children and cry out to God.
Gather them in your arms for they are the life of your love.
Some mornings will dawn bright even when some nights
    were cold and gray.
Gather in your arms the self you must now cherish.
Redeeming days are coming and truly they are on their
    way.
May it be our hope that children who admire doves will
    have a word to say.
I pray for you, my sister, though you are a whole world
    away.

LIVING ALONE BESIDE THE PHONE

People living alone and dying at home.
No one calling to see if they are gone.
Put it in check. Don't be fake.
There really is a lot at stake.
A little child living alone, all because her mother has died,
    And she doesn't understand that her mother is gone.
Hold on now, you've got to wait.
There was a friend who stopped by and discovered her fate.
True, this is the end of that tale.
Stay awhile and listen, for there are many more for sale.
The newspapers, magazines and screens are full of many
    gone lonely.
No one called and no one came by to say," I'll see you
    again another day."
No phone rings. No doorbell sounds.
Shut up and scared we are with unknown neighbors all
    around.
Who did we call today?
Who did we pray for today?
Who did we think about today?
Go, find a way.
Make this life matter.
Have a word to say.
Share a smile.
Share a meal.
Share a dollar.
Find a who.
After all, one day it may be me or it may be you.
So put it out there.
Spread it around.
What goes up and out may one day on our doorstep come
    back down.

If not to us, then to one who needs to know the truth that is
     true.
Here's love looking at love when love is looking at you.
Some spread hate, and it's out there.
Choose to spread love, sharing and caring.
Answer the call to stand and be daring.
Acknowledge our neighbors of the second command.
The ones we see revealed by the one with the nail prints in
     His hands.

TELL SOMEONE

Coming away from sorrow.
Shedding the burdens of grief.
A day full of sunshine, far past belief.
Coming away from sorrow as others have paved the way.
Breathe deep the air of this dawning day.
Not one thing to count as shame.
The pain has actually been gain.
View of the world around, breaking forth in much clearer
     light.
Tell someone else this one day they'll experience when life
     again flows nearer to right.

Doesn't seem possible at the beginning, to possess sanity
     and compassion at the end.
No, not now. No, not then.
Doesn't seem possible by day or by night.
Tell them and pray for them.
You now know it's true.
Never forget to pass on the message that was given to you.
Many said the words right out of their mouths.
My prayers will ascend for you.
This journey will take a while.

Chapter Four

REFLECTIONS

The time comes when quiet meanderings of the mind cause you to question every thought, belief and action you ever had, as though you wish to be purged of the silliness of life. This fourth grouping of poems came about as I was arranging the order of poems in each chapter. Several poems ultimately reflect an acquired wisdom, while others simply express passion.

When the broken pieces at the bottom of your heart begin to heal and you've allowed joy to come back into your life, the grief periods continue to impact you. Many perspectives you hold dear have changed. People begin to matter more than things or ideologies. You sense the need to avoid rushes to judgement. In other words, your value system has become tempered by your grief experience. A new and deeper understanding of the teachings from the Bible about the supreme importance of unselfish love, first for God and then for your neighbor as yourself emerges. A more thorough understanding regarding the identity of the "neighbor" whom God's Word admonishes us to love as ourselves evolves. And because we have felt God hold us so close to Him in abounding love during our struggle, we gain a greater understanding of how His love supercedes all of our manmade divisions. This fresh view of life can propel you forward through the rest of your life.

Hopefully, the grief experience engenders within us a greater desire to fully enjoy, each day, the gifts we already have from the hand of God. Being able to appreciate and share the awesome wonder and beauty of our existence is a gift in itself.

The thoughts in the poems that poured through my mind for this chapter gave rise to me reading and meditating on the following scriptures. "For God speaketh once, yea twice, yet man perceiveth it not" (Job 33:14). Much of the wisdom we gain comes from difficult experiences, which we probably could avoid, if only we were more perceptive of the voice of God. The second verse establishes a very apparent message. "If a man say, I love God, and hateth his brother, he is a liar: for he that loveth not his brother whom he hath seen, how can he love God whom he hath not seen?" (I John 4:20).

THINKING ALONE

Living alone now, with empty time to think.
Long before life swims over its brink.
So today, here is the thought.
So true, came right out of the blue.
Jesus wouldn't deface people, and neither should you.
No more shall I. That scar over my life is banished, no
    more to rise in strife.
Think about it. Give it some time.
Unclutter the hatred from our thoughts and the anger from
    our minds.
Life's a vapor, a mist, a puff of smoke.
Pack in some love.
Overflow in its healing emotion.
Create some dialogues.
Before, alone and thinking about the late hour of wasted
    devotions.
Change now.
Command the power before the power of hate signals too
    late.

Why are we content to point and stare?
Why are we so self-righteous and content without deep
    repair?
What to say?
What's not to say?
What to pray?
What's not to pray?
Swing open the doors.
Knock down the walls.
Reverse the pews.
From the fields for harvest,
Heed the call to choose.

BEFORE DEATH

It was too late.
The die had been cast.
A story had been told.
It was too late; life was too cold.
What could have been done?
You missed every clue.
Eyes on self, and not on you.

Eyes from self to near.
Not enough vision to see the weary tear.
Face tired, body weak and stooped.
Steps slow, hands feeble, nothing new.
Look now harder and clearer.
Feel it, tell it, tongue do not be still.
Someone may hear.
Someone may show what their heart says they know.
Grow before death, unbidden, walks in an open door.

A TENDER SHOOT

Gave his life in war.
Sacrificed his young blood in war.
Honored his country in war.
Speaks no more in life.
Embraces no more his wife.

Said goodbye to his dad.
Gave a treasured hug to his mom.
Saluted his brother.
Told his sister to stay strong.
No one knew then that he would be gone this long.
Not even the chaplain who heard the witness and accep-
    tance of Christ in his song.
He shot and they shot.
Two shots fired.
Two homes now bereft.
Two tender shoots have died.
One for each side.

WONDERFUL THIS FREEDOM

The ways of the Lord in the wise man's eyes are wonderful.
He sought it, and was led to freedom.
Truth, indeed, set his understanding free.
How?
He acknowledged the truth of the matters of life.
Some he saw were large.
Some he saw were small.
They equaled the same.
Freedom on the other side of life's equation was their
     name.

Find it as precious as gold.
Love it for the sum of the story it holds.
Possess it and treasure it as silver.
Tighten your grip, not allowing a mite to slip.
Learn the way of truth and walk therein.
The light it shines on us, in us, and for us, yields freedom
     from sin.
It comes from a place once bidden and known.
A place our inner heart knows as our true home.
Who we are and are meant to be, truth does set us free.
So said the wise men when writing to me.

A CHILD'S PLAY

Sometimes when your heart feels as though it's breaking in
    two,
A child will do a somersault just to bring joy to you.
How do they know how to make laughter real?
Time and again it's been said, they listen to the angels in
    their heads.

They ask about an elder and say, " let's give them a call."
Or they ask to visit so they can skip between their walls.
When the news arrives that the same elder you called or
    visited, from earth has closed their eyes,
You wonder, how did a happy child know that it was time
    to spread cheer before a soul walked out the door?
Has to be the angels in their heads and the obedience in
    their hearts,
Which make their lines in the play of life the grandest parts.

PICKING AND CHOOSING

Can't do anything about dying days.
Just a moment in time when the final clock chimes.
Not a day given to choice.
The ground may not even be moist.
Just a day like any other.
May be rainy, may be sunny, could be full of fun.
Unknown, even when known for very long.
Always suspected but not truly expected.
Not given a chance to do what we wouldn't do.
Not given a chance to do that which we would.
No picking and no choosing.
Treasure today what one day we'll be losing.

LIFE'S BIG BUBBLE

Such a bubble, such a burst of living light in vapored mirth.
Completely enclosed, but do not touch.
It is just a bubble; it is just a burst.

If only there were senses so exquisitely refined.
If only there were fences so impenetrably entwined.
If only such dewdrops were stretched for permanence in
     time.

Pop! There goes life.
Into a million escaping rainbows.
Floating to join a billion vapors.
Merging onto another dew bubbled leaf.
In another valley, beyond another mountain peak.
Hope! To see this bubble live life again.
Ensnaring and caressing.
While capturing the eye for a visual blessing.
Look and view living dew.
Fragile beauty designed just for you.

Be quick to regard, within your own backyard.
Such a bubble.
Such a burst.
Oh, what mirth!
Pop!

SELF

Too into self to view the worlds on the shelf.
Life now pulled along.
Life that was once strong.
Regain the hill.
Climb. Heart be still.

Take more time.
Savor the flavor.
Smell the roses.
Gather a bouquet, thorns and all.
Let their full pleasure enthrall.
Why did it take so long to learn?
Why did wisdom have to arrive in this way?
All because of that agonizing day.

Now grass is green.
Now trees touch the sky.
Now rivers gurgle as they flow.
Oceans gleam as smooth blue glass.
The sky is really blue. Not scientific; just blue.
Butterflies are flying sculptures of art.
Red birds, blue birds, black birds, brown birds chirp their
    colors.
Listen.
The flowers of the field dressed in style, invite us to sit and
    enjoy their colorful smiles.
Never saw all this before.
Not until death entered and opened that door.

GET OUT OF TOWN

The wind blew hard.
The rain fell fast and steady.
The river and the ocean roared signaling that they, too,
    were ready.
Then the great waters rose and flooded the land.
And many stood bewildered with no money or tickets in
    hand.
They'd told them to get out of town.
But how? In what?
They told them to go.
Somebody just didn't know.
Many didn't know.
They knew not how and not with what.

There existed a warning answered by the conjunction but.
Now they are finally gone; some near home.
Some out and about and far away.
Some at home where again they stay.
None able to forget that awful day.

Forget that day in August.
Can't because the storm and the ignorance of who we are
    bought us.
Bought those with power who make rules.
Bought those who are poor and those who had to choose.
Bought those with kind hearts who didn't know the reality
    of life in those parts.
That our country needs more caring and a lot more sharing.

Found out floodwaters wash and winds reveal, baring for
    all the world to see the real that is real.
Daring us to love before it's too late.
Daring us to give up the excuses and the hate.
Daring us to be what those with the light claim.
Look out and see and lift the shame.
In a land called plenty, how the Word gets heard
comes through the water, the wind and the flood.

SLAY THEM

One by one count until it's done.
Name the widows, orphans too.
Time grows the roll.
When it ends, it swells again.
Slay them in revenge.
One by one, count until it's done.
Name the widows, the orphans too.
Time grows this roll.
Write it on the scroll.
When it ends, let's begin again.

Dare ask the question?
Dare answer it, too?
Either me, either you?
What if they gave a war and no one came?
The answer could mean names on the roll as intended by
    and by.
Correct! I want to believe your reply is right.
Even though whenever death comes, it steals as a thief in
    the night.

HELLO WORLD!

Hello world. Are you out there?
Why?
Ask the right questions. Get the right answers.
Maybe.
Why maybe? Why not yes? There are too many no's.
That, I know.
I'd like to know yes for a change..
What are you asking?
Hello, world. Stay out there. Don't walk away.
There might not be another day to think this over.
Not another day to smell sweet clover.
Move over. Make room.
Stick around. See what's soon to come and soon to go.
Soon to say, no more, no more.
Maybe tomorrow, we can win this.
Win what?
A chance to be friends. A chance to start again.
A chance to say no to war. A chance to say yes to love.
A chance to say no to jealousy. A chance to say no to hate.
Ask the right questions. Give the right answers.
Stay out there; it's never too late.
World, are you out there?
Brave and not afraid?
This can be the start. This can be the day.
Stick around. Don't walk away.
Not until the answers shine forth as the noonday sun.
It's possible to make this the one.
Chance now to answer. Chance now to change.
Chance now to shower the earth with cleansing rain.
To make clean, to wash away,
To prepare a place for that which others once did slay.
Love, peace, hope, calm, and joy, here and now.
By hook, by crook, by still waters deep,

Love we can hold and love we can keep,
For the beauty of a radiant day, for the peace of a starry
    night.
For a way to make wrong things right.
Where are you?
World, are you out there?

Chapter Five

ACCEPTING JOY

B e assured that the day will come when the joy of living returns as a dear treasure. This final chapter is reserved for joy as a tribute to honor the love that our loved ones had for us and what they would want to witness us experiencing in our lives.

One day I realized that writing poetry was my way of journaling. I actually tried to keep a journal. It was the suggestion of a grief counselor. A friend agreed and even bought me a journal to use. Writing a journal though, just wasn't me. I couldn't stick to it. What was happening, and eventually became very helpful, were the poems that would flow through my head constantly. They so aptly described how I was feeling and my views about my experiences. Somehow the poems served as a cathartic release of the searing grief that never left my mind. In verse, I could express my fears, why I was crying, how I didn't understand how to live without my husband, or just that I was in so much emotional pain. With each poem, it was as if another footstep was taken forward on my journey of finding peace.

Ultimately, this journey brought me to a point in my altered life where I knew I now had the power to accept joy. Joy was now available but it was also a choice.

The verse of scripture that I believe characterizes this final chapter of poems comes from the book of Nehemiah. "Then he said unto them, Go your way, eat the fat, and drink the sweet, and send portions unto them for whom nothing is prepared: for this day is holy unto our Lord: neither be ye sorry: for the Joy of the Lord is your strength" (Nehemiah 8:10).

WELCOME JOY

Go ahead, let joy in.
Go ahead, it's time for its emotion to win.
So many days it's lingered outside.
So many tears have kept it away.
Now the weeping tears have said goodbye.
Recognize the dawning of a bright new sky.

What awaits is not totally new, just finally acceptable for
     you to be you.
The you that can laugh fully and without reserve.
The you that can accept the happiness that you deserve.
Reclaim the you that brightens at the sound of the laughter
     of children at play.
Allow the happiness of this awakening moment.
Don't let it pass; permit it to stay.

Shout out to joy and say you are welcome to come inside.
I claim you. I accept you.
Joy, hold my hand and be my guide.
Escort me out of this cocoon of sorrow.
Help me fit my wings and sail to my tomorrow.
Just as you showed me how to put my smile back on my
     face.
Thank you for escorting me away from Satan's taunts of
     disgrace.

PEACE

Welcome peace that passes all understanding.
Come now joy, quick and demanding.
Fill to overflowing the beauty of a new flower ever
    changing and growing.
His peace he gives, not as the world but as the water of life
    from the well.
His peace he gives as he prays and makes intercession.
His peace is a gift for he has seen and known the many
    tears of sorrow.
He too wept as he gave of his peace for the joy of an eternal
    tomorrow.

NO SHAME TO MAKE JOY

Come away from sorrow.
Shed the burdens of grief.
Enjoy days full of sunshine that are far past belief.
Come away from sorrow.
So many others have paved the way and bid you come.
Breathe deeply the air of the dawn of your new day.

Count nothing as shame.
Your pain has actually been gain.
Not so at the beginning.
Not even a thought.
Learned a lot and lived through much.
Come out of sorrow and get back in touch.

Bear no shame that sorrow bowed you down.
Bear not the shame by which many have been bound.
Let no one mark your path and order your boundaries set.
Life has always been more than just a test.
Life is a lesson to be lived and a journey to explore.
Nothing less and nothing more.
Come away from sorrow with new views from which to
      choose.
Come away from sorrow now worth more than you will
      ever lose.
Tell someone else torn with grief that this one day, they
      too, will do.
Probably doesn't seem possible to them here and now.
So you must tell them.
To them nothing seems right.
Not by the brightest light of day or the brightest moon of
      night.
Tell them and pray for them.
You know it's true.

The promise of a better day about which others assured
you.
Tell them about shame: Accept no shame. Give no shame.
Call it by its name.
It's sorrow and it hurts. You are saddened and you feel
much pain.
That morning of triumphant joy will come as a day that
stands upon nights of weeping.
That day of coming away from sorrow.
That day of healing, within the joy and blessing of a bright
tomorrow.

PRAYER FOR JOY IN THE MORNING

Many are the things that we just don't know.
Many are the ways that we may not grow.
Size this up and size it down.
A smile is a replacement for a frown.

Somebody tried because somebody knew.
All about the sadness that pierced you through and through.
One day they hoped that it would come.
A rainbow they prayed for you to enjoy with the noon day
     sun.

Oh sure, we think that nothing like that exists.
But don't forget that many prayers create a sweet smelling
     mist.
Reaching heavenward, they are bound to bear fruit
Harvesting the joy that's meant for you.
Allow entrance into your heart.
Cringe not in diminished faith.
Accept this pleasure which desires to stay.

CANDY FUN
(Because our loved ones would want us to laugh again)

Seldom good for you they say, though attractive in red and
   blue.
Go ahead, add yellow and green.
It doesn't matter if you are seen.
But why would you go ahead and try?
Beware of the seducing ones.
Spiral in shape or round in form.
You want two but start with one.
Then when in your mouth it melts,
Loosen your resolve and let out your belt.
Why of course it's candy.
Thank you for one but give me another just for fun.

HARBINGER OF SPRING

True harbinger of Spring, I heard you ring.
With a voice so clear and a song so near.
Just as the dawn was lifting its face,
You took to your wings with a sweet melody in place.
Year after year, you visit outside our cold windowpanes.
With your call, you awaken us to hear the joy and warmth
    of Spring's promise.

The flowers are coming, you do sing aloud.
The showers are coming to make our gardens proud.
How do you know so much? Who sends you our way?
God, in his love and mercy, you did say.
I can see it now, and I can smell it too.
Beautiful skies that follow the chill morning dew.
Giving way to sunshine, giving way to joy.

Keep singing that song.
Keep summoning us along.
Messages in verses you sing in golden keys.
Now is the time to enjoy day while it does linger.
Now is the time to look and see the beauty near and even
    far away.
Never waits for you.
Never know when the song of Spring for you will be no
    more.

So sing on harbinger and make the announcement clear.
Your message in song of the days to come is a welcome joy
    that we hold dear.
Our weary cold homes await to hear the song you'll sing.
We awaken from sleep and slumber, stretching out our
    woes with the smiles you bring.
Sing loud, sing proud, awaken the neighborhood.

Ring in the news of soft and lovely days to come with your
  melodic hymn.

Keep singing, most people say, for they are yearning to
  experience the delights
of beautiful, lazy summer days and starlit summer nights.
Yearning swells within to welcome love in the parks on a
  stroll or at a picnic on a grassy knoll.
We visualize happy children outside at play.
We imagine their merry laughter as they swing and sway.

Dear harbinger, do you realize how grand is your voice of
  happiness?
Sing on and proclaim your announcement again.
We love to listen long before the alarm clock's bell has
  anything to say.
Sing on and make the announcement clear.
Your song of the days to come is a welcome joy that we
  hold dear.

NO KIDDING

What do little children know?
How do they know what they know?
In many ways they reveal their intellect.
They observe, they hear, they repeat.
They watch you take your seat.
Then they claim their chance to stand and show.
Some action they have watched and learned, sometimes
    fast and sometimes slow.
Taking turn after turn to accomplish their feat.
Some word you said and forgot, from their innocent mouths
    they will repeat.
Then comes those times of no precedent set, when their
    actions will take away your breath.
They may turn their head upside down and give a smile that
    brightens a sad, sad frown.
Witness them running back and forth again and again while
    stealing a look at you to see,
If with their energetic sprinting they've succeeded.
Doing their best to bring laughter and joy deep within your
    troubled heart.
How do they know that their cute antics you needed?
How do they know to do it over and over?
Driving out the pain by filling your joy to overflowing.

We say if only we had their energy.
They say they have energy to share for the happiness it
    brings.
For the smile they put on our face.
For the song we, again, find the peace to sing.

Dear little child, thank you so much.
Thank you for sharing the Master's touch.
Thank you for reaching into sorrow and pulling out
     gladness.
With your little strength and relentless vision,
You kept at it until you won the mustard seed decision.
We called it young energy.
You called it joy and play, with gleeful repetition.
Or maybe you were playing with your angels.
Whatever it took, someone was determined for you to fulfill
     a joyful mission.

Somehow, little children know who's sad.
What we once knew.
Think back to a time long gone.
When we, too, sang the silly little song.
Skipped left, then right all day long.
Some glad heart we made.
While someone alone and sad sat watching in the shade.
Now we understand what we did.
So let a kid be a kid.

WORDS TODAY

If only time could be rewound while time still goes ahead,
    then you would hear what I have heard said.
That little boy is little no more. That little footprint finder
    has stepped on ahead and out the door.
Have a share of the new words he has said.

Relegate
Replicate
Recoup
Reestablish
Replete
Relentless pursuit
Relinquish
Reciprocate
Restructure
Resilient.
Resurrect
A new generation, he's even started.
Graduated from college.
Invested, divested and working his smartest.
Actually heard you when you said, " Make a career boy out
    of what's in your head."

THANKSGIVING

On this Thanksgiving Day, be quiet and listen, a little child
   has much to say.
She announces, in her most commanding voice, that on this
   day we have a choice.
Be thankful and remember the ones who gave us life, the
   loving husband and the beautiful wife.
No longer here for her ever to touch and hold but with her
   words, her command to remember is sure and bold.

Some laugh and snicker that one so young on Thanksgiving
   Day has decided to explain.
It's not just about the delights on the table and the extra
   pounds we're sure to gain.
She reveals that it's also about the ones, now gone, who
   made us able to gather, to pray and prepare a feast.

From where did such a speech in one so young come?
It caught everyone off guard, even her Mom.
What dreams had she had? What visions did she
   understand?
In her heart beats sincere love for those about whom she
   speaks.
She didn't get to meet them. About them, she has been told.
What's her age?
Only five years old.

WHAT'S IN THE LAUGHTER?

What is it about a child's laughter?
Just one of those sweet moments in life that bursts forth the
moment after.
Hear now and laugh in your heart.
Don't let the innocence of such joy quickly depart.
Hold it for as long as you can.
A child's laughter is a song for every woman and man.
Maybe we've forgotten the power and the peace of
laughter.
Maybe we've forgotten how to laugh.

In the laughter of a child can be found the thrill of life in
gleeful sounds.
Unhindered by cares and uninhibited by rules and stares,
their laughter announces joy.
The joy may come from the freedom they feel in skipping
and twisting from left to right.
Something we find them willing to do, even in the darkest
of nights.
Their laughter may remind us of the joy that comes from
singing the words to a nursery school song.
Great bursts of laughter come forth, at times, from the
blowing of the wind on their face.
At other times, it may come from the exhilaration of
coming in first or last in a playful race.
Their merry laughter may spill forth from receiving a treat
or seeing bright-colored cars race by in the street.
Picking pretty flowers or lying in the grass, with laughter a
child displays how to take time to enjoy the beauty of
life before it's all past.

Let a child's merry voice of unbridled laughter sound.
Let its spirited echo lead the way around.
Around the toils and trials of a day too long.
Around the frayed nerves about to be sprung.
A child's laughter beckons smiles to replace frowns.
A child's laughter is medicine around which a troubled
heart can be unwound.

Imagine a green, flower-filled meadow full of laughing
children.
Imagine their sounds of laughter in the air as though it's
gold and silver.
Relax your mind, lower your shoulders, and turn your ears
to listen.
Allow yourself to shed the burdens of rage.
Throw your head back and laugh out loud.
Try it now, whether alone or in a crowd.
Doesn't matter where, doesn't matter when.
Laugh some more and laugh again.
See that child now stopping to smile.
Knowing their work of generating happiness may endure
for a while.
You owe them thanks.
The best thanks to give, is the laughter that journeys back
to their happy little ears.

A THING OF BEAUTY

Ever felt a rose petal or a butterfly's wing?
Ever heard the red robin sing?
Ever counted leaves of clover?
Ever smelled honeysuckle before you walked closer?
How about the roped beauty of a rainbow in the sky?
Or the pleasure that a clear babbling brook gives to the eye?
Now what's your thing of beauty that you wish to add?
There's more than enough to fill up each of our pads.
Go ahead and try your hand at writing a few.
Creation's astounding beauty offers many delights to
        inspire you.

DARK REACHES

Been in the darkest reaches of a nightmare.
Now coming out, now coming home.
Finally see light.
Finally see day.
Finally see noon.
Finally free to see a way.
A way to walk, though not run.
Not running away.
Can't risk losing what's been learned.
Can't risk losing what's been earned.
Earned the right to learn again.
To smile again.
To love again.
To define self again.
Know that such a nightmare can be survived.
Know that such a dawn will arrive.
What you've earned, and what you've learned, contain the
   journey's reward.
Permission has been granted to go make a great day and a
   brand new start.

It's true that you could not imagine living life when it did
   not matter.
Time has come to breathe in again and know the soreness
   has gone.
Breathe in again and accept that you are not alone.
In the shadow of the wings of God, your world awaits you.
Sample the tastes and delights with strength and no more
   fright.

Sure, there are things to be careful about.
There are fears strong and stout.
Breathe in and feel the wholeness.
Experience the new boldness.
There exists a you again.

Emerging now is a different you, a stronger you, born from
    this experience.
Truly, the half scar is still there, but it no longer caves in
    with every puff of air.
Go on now. Take your place.
Join with renewed vigor the world of your race.
Feels okay to return now without taking a bow.
Made tough decisions while in that nightmare.
Made bad decisions.
Cried many tears.
Almost gave up sometimes.
Prayed most times.
Sang old songs of Zion.
Learned and sang new ones, too.
Wrote poems.
Kept a journal.
Went to work.

Drove long journeys on short roads.
Drove short journeys alone on long roads.
Welcomed and held the babies of the next generations.
Moved away, and sometimes lost the way.

Saw reality looking into your eyes.
Adjusted to reality by making a way in the new life given.
Time has come to let go.
Grief periods, whether long or short, provide the needed
    time to adjust our hearts.
A place to hide out.
A place to hide wherein you may cry and scream.
A place to review your life's scenes.

It's okay to start anew.
Come on out of the cocoon of this dream-filled nightmare.
Come on out of the cocoon of this evolutionary journey.
Emerge with the new understandings from the verses lived
    and revealed.
Spread your wings on the prayers ascending.
Fly in color and splendor.
Champions do that from window to window.

SUMMARY

How do you move from denial and anger through trying to bargain with God for the return of your loved one from the dead? How do you get past bouts of bitter depression? How do you accept joy and laughter again for more than a moment or two? You find the way. It exists. As a believer, I clung to God. I talked to God. I prayed. Others prayed for me. They talked to me. I listened to my pastor's sermons. I recalled the messages of previous sermons. I read the word of God.

Then there was this poetry. Through poetry, I found I was allowing God to lead me to find the way that would work best for me. The anguish, doubt, and pain were written before me and not left inside festering into insurmountable barriers to eventual healing.

As I wrote, I found that I was being reminded of God's promises. For each, seemingly debilitating emotion I recorded, I was often immediately reminded of a promise from God that expressed how much He loves me. One of those reminders that came most often was Jesus' passion for us shown by His death on the cross and by His resurrection from the dead. That would always lead to my recalling that He now sits at the right hand of God making intercession for us. I felt reassured that I would make it through this. It might be overwhelming at times, but if I maintained my faith and stayed within God's loving arms, I would survive.

Nothing characterizes what I learned from viewing life from a window of grief better than two quotes I read in a daily devotional published for Cedine Bible Mission by Walk Thru The Bible

97

Ministries, Inc. The first one appeared on May 26, 2007. "Suffering can produce great depths of character, mature understanding, warm compassion, and rich spirituality." The second one is from May 31, 2007. "Pray for a faith that will not shrink when washed in the waters of affliction." Just as I was finishing the writing of this book, these two quotes were listed in the margins of the daily readings. The quotes felt very familiar to me. The poems I wrote expressed similar lessons that I had learned. Trials will come but through prayer and supplication; we can hold on to our faith that God actually has it all under control. He desires to bring us to a place of greater awareness of his abiding love.

In this same devotional, the readings for the last 14 days at the end of May were taken from the book of Job. Again, nothing could have been more providential than finding all these together at just the right time. I thought of a question I would like to ask Job. The question would be, "Job, how did you do this?" In other words, "Job, how did you suffer such great losses and experience such trials and still maintain your sanity and your faith?" Many of us actually know the answer to that question by what we have heard preached and what we have read in the book of Job. Often, what is missing is our having an understanding based on our going through a similar situation. When I studied those last 14 lessons and searched through Job again after writing this poetry, I discovered that I had a better understanding of the book of Job simply because I now had my own heat-wrenching grief experience.

Something else that absolutely stopped me in my tracks was a verse of scripture from Job 19:23, where Job says, "Oh that my words were now written! Oh that they were printed in a book!" I don't know how many seconds or maybe even minutes passed before I realized that I was reading and rereading this one verse over and over. The message of these words was clear and affirming to my mission. Since these poems had been my way of working through my journey of grief, I, too, understood that there is a blessed relief in using words to express and release the gut-wrenching pain of sorrow. It occurred to me almost immediately that I now had a better understanding of the book of Job simply because I had recorded my experiences through these poems. Not only did I have a written record, I had a record to compare. I was able to see in my own responses, a kinship to Job's record of what he had endured.

This is a journey that can produce a more mature, caring, understanding and joyful person. That may be hard to believe but think of it as an experience that can help you find great delight as you do when you see beautiful, flowering morning glories break open in bloom on a sunny day. Yes, we know night is coming and that night just left, but while it's day and we have a chance to witness the exquisite beauty of the faithful morning glory, we marvel at its freshness and promise. Each day, beauty will come. We just have to begin opening our minds to grasp and appreciate all the goodness and joy that surrounds us when it's present.

Through the various poems of this book, I have opened my heart to share the pain, sadness, difficulties, triumphs and the turning away from self-pity and doubt. I feel very strongly that it is in our acknowledging our weakness and crying out to God that He is most able to capture our attention and make us strong.

If my being open and vulnerable in laying bare my struggle with the pain of grief as a believer, has helped one person who questioned why they just couldn't seem to get past overbearing sorrow, I consider the mission of this book accomplished. Have faith that eventual healing will come. As you make your way toward that day, please know that someone understands and cares about your sad heart. There is no magic formula that sets a time limit or that states we all grieve in the same way. We can be encouraged though to know that if others have made it through, we can too. That is why I selected to end this book with the following scripture verse:

"Blessed be God, even the Father of our Lord Jesus Christ, the Father of mercies, and the God of all comfort; Who comforted us in all our tribulation, that we may be able to comfort them which are in any trouble, by the comfort wherewith we ourselves are comforted of God" (IICorinthians 1:3-4).

Printed in the United States
107685LV00004B/481-519/A